Locally known as Patwa, the Kwéyòl language comes from an influence of mainly French but also English, Spanish and African native languages. Having many similarties to other varieties of Creole, spoken in countries such as, Haiti, Martinique and Guadeloupe, this strand of Creole is mainly spoken in the sister islands of Saint Lucia and Dominica.

This series of books seeks to preserve the deep cultural essence of the Kwéyòl language and it's influence for furture generations. Within this book you will find the Kwéyòl alphabet, a list of every day Kwéyòl terms and the English translation. Each page includes a description of the correct pronounciation of each letter, a Kwéyòl word and an image to develop you and your family's Kwéyòl.

A
Sounds like the **a** in **a**pple

Abiyé

To dress

B

Sounds like the **b** in **b**oat

Bouwik

Donkey

Ch

Sounds like the <u>sh</u> in <u>sh</u>ip

Chyen

Dog

D

Sounds like the <u>d</u> in <u>d</u>oor

Dwèt

Finger

Dj
Sounds like the **j** in **j**ump

Djòl

Snout or mouth of an animal.

É

Sounds like the **e** in gr**e**y

Ékwi

To write

È

Sounds like the **e** in l**e**t

Èskoupyon

Scorpion

F

Sounds like the **f** in **f**riend

Fanm

Woman

G

Sounds like the **g** in **g**irl

Gason

Son, Boy

H

Sounds like the **h** in **h**ouse

Hach

Axe

I

Sounds like the **ee** in gr**ee**n

Lamouwi

Saltfish

J

Sounds like the **s** in lei**s**ure

Jako

St Lucian Parrot

K

Sounds like the **k** in **k**ite

Kat

The number 4

L

Sounds like the **l** in **l**ake

Liv

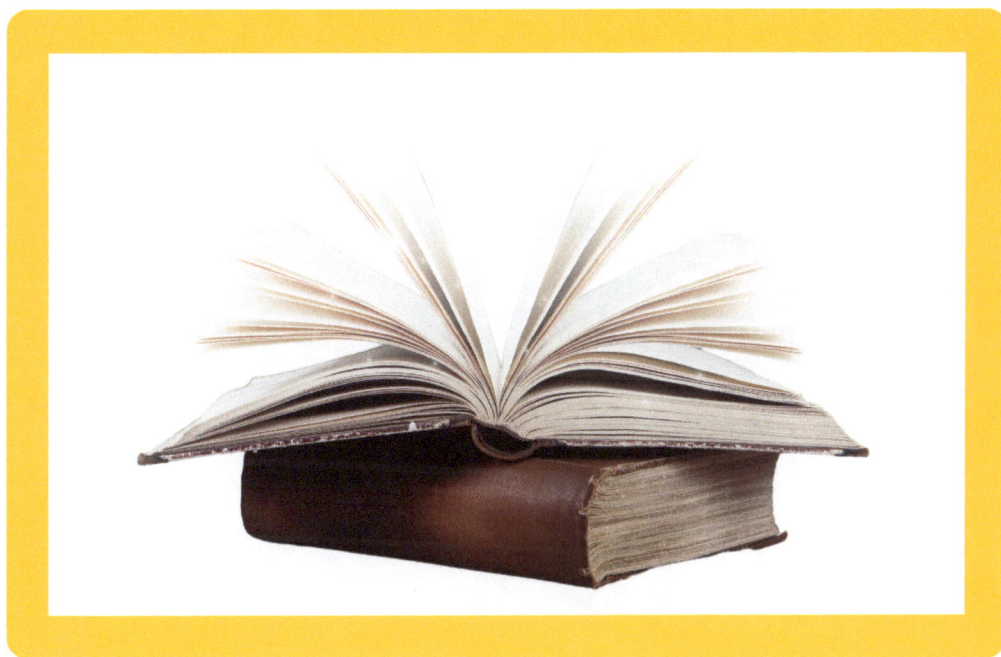

Book

M

Sounds like the **m** in **m**other

Mouton

Sheep

N

Sounds like the **n** in **n**est

Nich

Nest

Ng

Sounds like the **ng** in ri**ng**

Zonng

Nail

Ò

Sounds like the **aw** in L**aw**n

Òswè

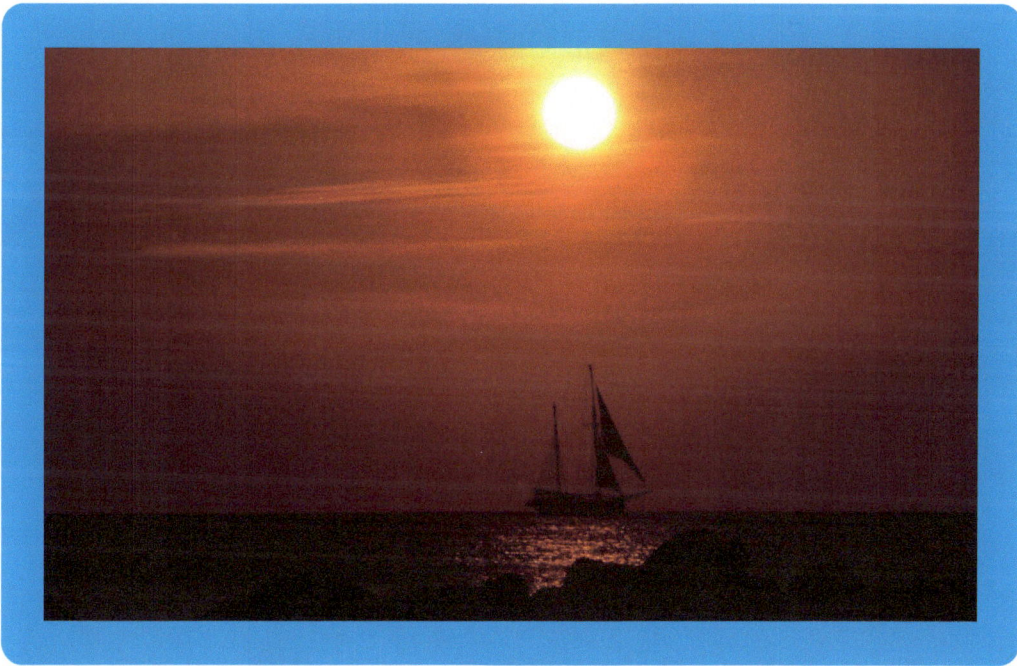

Evening

O

Sounds like the **o** in r**o**pe

Obliyè

To forget

Ou

Sounds like the **u** in r**u**ler

Ouvè

To open

P

Sounds like the **p** in **p**eople

Patat

Potato

R

Sounds like the **r** in **r**ed

Radyo

Radio

s

Sounds like the **s** in **s**tar

Souwi

Mouse

T

Sounds like the **t** in **t**able

Tonton

Uncle

Tj

Sounds like the **ch** in **ch**air

Tjè

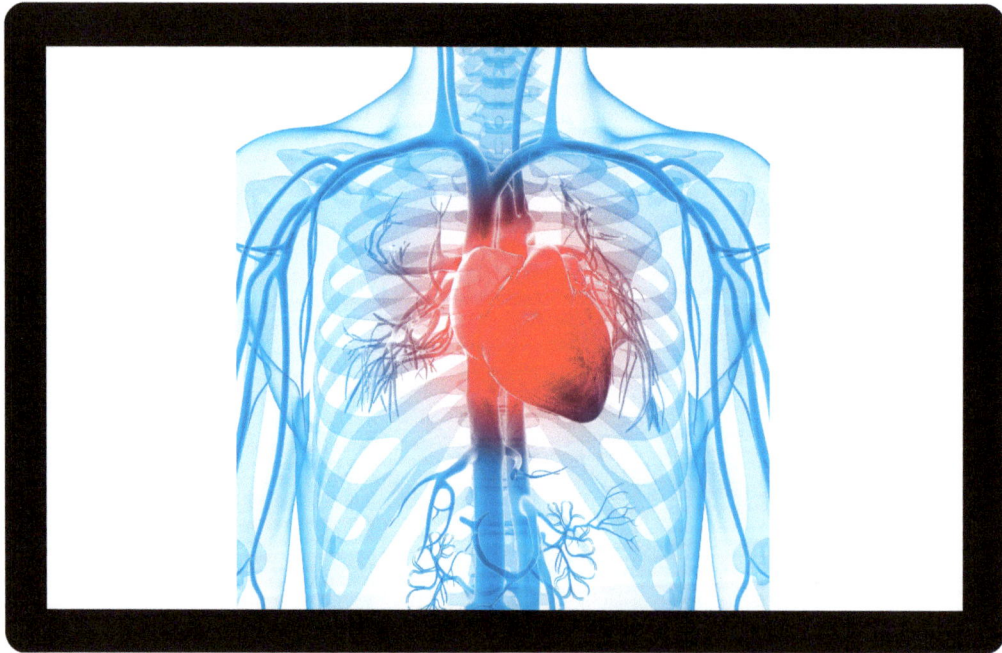

Heart

V

Sounds like the **v** in **v**an

Volan

Flying Fish

W

Sounds like the <u>w</u> in <u>w</u>eb

Wavèt

Cockroach

Y

Sounds like the y in yes

Yamn

Yam

Z

Sounds like the **z** in **z**ebra

Zé

Egg

Nasal Vowels

Nasal vowels are pronounced by passing air through the nose and mouth.

An

An is a nasal sounding **A**
Sounds like the **aun** in **aun**t

Anwajé

Angry

En

En is a nasal sounding **E**

Sounds like the **en** **i**n the French word **en**trée

Endé

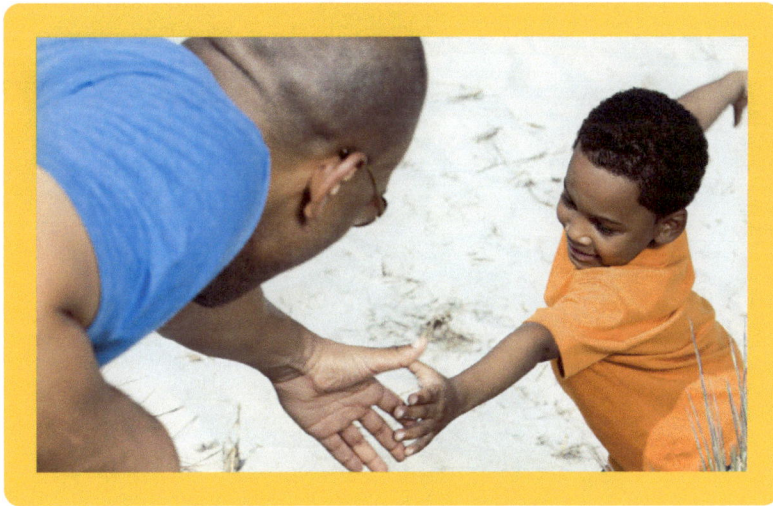

To Help

On

On is a nasal sounding **O**
Sounds like the **o** in l**o**ng

Onnèt

Honest

Numbers

Limowo

One fish

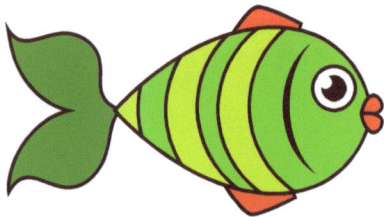

Yonn pwéson

1   Yonn

Two birds

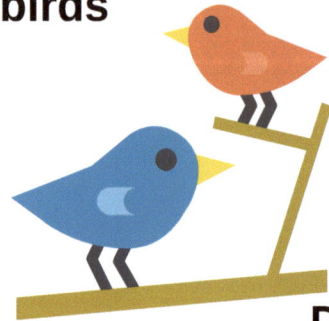

De jibyé

2   Dé

Three caterpillars

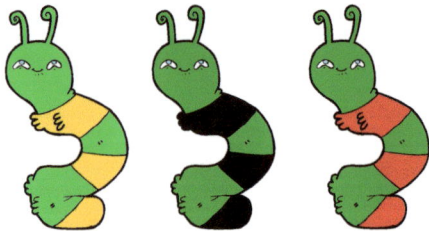

Twa chini

3   Twa

Four dogs

Kat chyen

4   Kat

Five loaves of bread

Senk pen

5   Senk

Six mangoes

Sis mango

6   Sis

Seven papayas or pawpaw

Sèt papay

7   Sèt

Eight bananas

Ywit fig

8   Ywit

Nine boys

Nèf gason

9 Nèf

Ten girls

Dis tifi

10 Dis

Other books in this series:

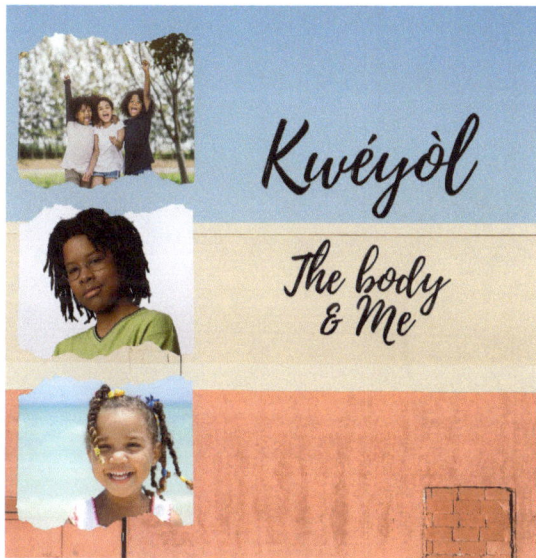

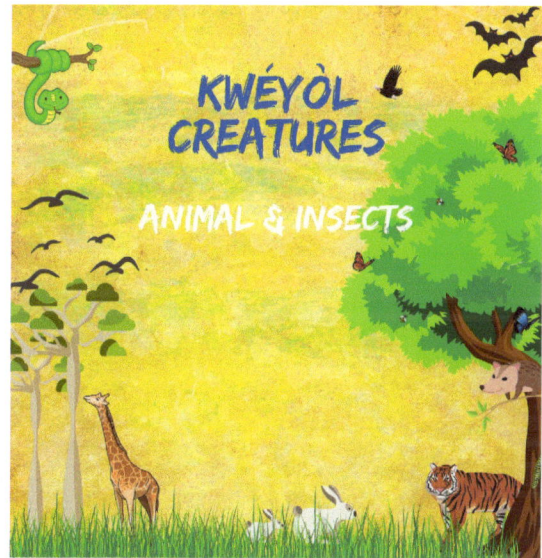

More books coming soon

Black Gold Publishing

Black Gold Publishing

www.ingramcontent.com/pod-product-compliance
Lightning Source LLC
Chambersburg PA
CBHW041429090426
42741CB00003B/97

9 781838 213404